The Other White People

From Vikings to Russians

By

RODERICK EDWARDS

Copyright © 2022

rodericke.com/white

INTRODUCTION

So many topics have become taboos or immediate cause for complete cancellation of the person that dares to broach them, so that many productive discussions are left unsaid. Race is such a pariah subject unless you have been given the societal nod as a member of a marginalized group that by the sheer tint of your skin, allows you to talk about race issues without challenge.

Being white is automatically equated to European colonialism that not only brought black Africans to the New World in chains but knowingly and unwittingly decimated the native population of the Americas through theft, war, and disease.

But there are entire nations of white people that were never part of this blight in human history. In fact, much of what has been laid upon the shoulders of English-speaking white people was the dominion of the olive-skinned Spanish and Portuguese two-hundred years before the British, French, Dutch, and other Europeans even set foot on American shores.

This book is not going to attempt to justify real racism or actual deplorable human behavior, however nor will this book shy away from investigating and revealing the truth.

Table of Contents

DEDICATION

To aunt Dolores whom I only knew a short time after finally finding you fifty years into my physical life. We'll meet again, I'm certain.

CHAPTER 1 THE OTHERS

The author of this book is an adoptee and as such, has the unique perspective of all adoptees of being an outsider to even their own heritage. This is especially true when speaking of an adoptee adopted by parents of a different race or nationality. The adoptee typically adapts to the adoptive parents culture and heritage but at some point attempts to better understand the culture and heritage of their biological ancestors.

The author's culture and heritage hails not only directly from Germany, as his biological father emigrated to the USA as a young boy, but also to Norway, to the homeplace of the Norse; the Vikings as the author has traced his biological maternal roots all the way back to 680AD in Norway.

Since the author is "white" and was adopted by white English-speaking parents, perhaps someone would claim he has no different culture and heritage to find as say would an Asian adoptee adopted by white (or black) American parents. But that is the very crux of this book; that white Anglo-Saxon or Gauls (French) for that matter are different than the *other* white people; the Vikings and Russians. Further, if the discussion is about Europeans, we should include Spanish and Portuguese into the group. History so often glosses over the fact that much of the New

World was colonized by the Spanish and Portuguese conquistadors. It presents the descendants of Spanish and Portuguese colonists as merely "Latinos" in contrast to Europeans, when in reality both are Europeans.

This book attempts to show the reader that despite the narrative of politics, there is another group of white people that had nothing to do with all the ills ascribed to white people by history books.

According to black nationalist leader, Elijah Muhammad as retold by Malcolm X, about sixty-six hundred years ago a black scientist with an unusually large head named Yacub was banished to the island of Patmos with 59,999 of his followers.

"Though he was a black man, Mr. Yacub, embittered toward Allah now, decided, as revenge, to create upon the earth a devil race-a bleached-out, white race of people.

From his studies, the big-head scientist knew that black men contained two germs, black and brown. He knew that the brown germ stayed dormant as, being the lighter of the two germs, it was the weaker.

Mr. Yacub, to upset the law of nature, conceived the idea of employing what we today know as the recessive genes structure, to separate from each other the two germs, black and brown, and then grafting the brown germ to progressively lighter, weaker stages. The humans resulting, he knew, would be, as they became lighter, and weaker, progressively also more susceptible to wickedness and evil. And in this way finally he would achieve the intended bleached-out white race of devils." – The Autobiography of Malcolm X, page 110 https://antilogicalism.com/wp-content/uploads/2018/04/malcom-x.pdf

The "Yacub History" as related by Elijah Muhammad and Malcolm X is given to contrast the account sometimes proclaimed by people that the white race is superior, simply by the anecdotal evidence of so many technological advancements by white cultures. The author wanted to immediately show that as outraged as the reader might become by the contents of this book, there are accounts just as wild and unfounded as anything the reader thinks they are about to experience. It is hoped that the reader will get beyond the conditioned urge to reject or see as racist, any discussion of race by a white person and instead embrace this discussion as a person looking at the anthropological data and letting it lead the way.

While it is highly unlikely any modern reader would believe the Yacub History as the origin of the white race, that account was presented as a serious "fact" and no doubt was a great influence on then Malcolm X who later recanted his tutelage under the Nation of Islam and took a more rational approach.

"While there is no doubt that Malcolm believed in the teachings of Elijah Muhammad with all his heart and all his soul for most of his adult life, namely, the belief that all whites were devils, it cannot be denied that his views about Caucasians evolved and that he eventually rejected them wholeheartedly." – Malcolm X: Message to Humanity, page 211
https://brill.com/view/book/edcoll/97890043086
88/B9789004308688-s010.xml

Does the reader find it odd that the author has decided to open this chapter with so much reference to a radical black activist?

The point of it is this, just as it took some time for Malcolm Little to become Malcolm X, then to become Malik El-Shabazz so too we need to be open to the fact that there are others – *other* white people that don't fit the narrative, not only of some justifiably angry black humans but also the misplaced narrative of politically opportunistic white humans trying to gain virtue or favor. Malcolm X understood how he was being used and how people are still being used today:

> **"The white liberal differs from the white conservative only in one way: the liberal is more deceitful than the conservative. The liberal is more hypocritical than the conservative. Both want power, but the white liberal is the one who has perfected the art of posing as the Negro's friend and benefactor; and by winning the friendship, allegiance, and support of the Negro, the white liberal is able to use the Negro as a pawn or tool in this political 'football game' that is constantly raging**

between the white liberals and white conservatives.

Politically the American Negro is nothing but a football and the white liberals control this mentally dead ball through tricks of tokenism: false promises of integration and civil rights. In this profitable game of deceiving and exploiting the political politician of the American Negro, those white liberals have the willing cooperation of the Negro civil rights leaders. These 'leaders' sell out our people for just a few crumbs of token recognition and token gains. These 'leaders' are satisfied with token victories and token progress because they themselves are nothing but token leaders." -- Malcolm X, https://www.globalresearch.ca/what-did-malcolm-x-really-think-about-the-democratic-party/5576198

This book is not primarily a political treatment, but despite that people try to separate politics from other facets of life, politics is merely human culture and so it permeates everything. It is best to understand politics relationship to the topic being discussed rather than to operate in a vacuum that ignores politics influence on any given discussion.

The politics that the author is trying to show is that talking about white people and their history immediately conjures accusations of white supremacy and connects that accusation to African slavery and the subjugation of Native American cultures. While it is politically acceptable to speak of "pride" when it comes to any other race than white people, it will cause immediate pushback from across the political spectrum for anyone to merely discuss a proud heritage that includes a predominately white culture. The politics of this topic are so heavy that a book like this would be out of the question to be read in the open air in most places. Try it. See what happens.

When we talk about the other white people, we could even include the Irish if we want to show a large segment of people that were also brought to the Americas as indentured servants and slaves. The Irish were not perpetrating the things for which most white people today are charged. But the author wanted to get even further away from Europe.

The image of Vikings is one of long-haired, bearded, axe-wielding warriors leaping from their ships onto the English shores of the Saxon Christians, at least that is how it is portrayed on TV and movies. The Norse or Viking culture is decidedly not historically European. Vikings were considered white "savages" and as uncivilized as the "Indians", or rather the aboriginal peoples of the Americas. Europeans didn't claim them. They were truly, the other white people.

Next, this book will introduce and detail the Russians or the Rus which originate among the larger white people group called *Slavs*. The Slavs originally inhabited the upper northern region of what has been known as the Soviet Union and in present time as Russia. While some references may include Slavs as Europeans, they more aptly fit into the archaic region of "Eurasia", just as does the Ukraine which has of late been called a European country.

This book is also not intending to be a geography primer but it is important that the reader understand the distinction of classifications. Reading our modern notions back into how these people groups saw themselves, deprives us of understanding them in their own context. Neither Vikings nor Russians saw themselves as Europeans. Calling them Europeans now has underlying political motivations which would become more obvious if the reader was so inclined to unpack that research.

So, here we have two people groups; the Vikings and the Russians but in fact they have similar roots. While the Vikings we often think about historically are the

Norse people, the Russians too are Vikings from the Kievan Rus. The Rus were ruled by Varangians which were Swedish Vikings that had settled in the region. (ref: https://en.wikipedia.org/wiki/Varangians)

Perhaps a better designation for these other white people could be *Scandinavians* which is inclusive of Northern Germany, Denmark, Sweden, Norway, and Finland and then as mentioned, by extension, Russia.

The question might be, why does it matter to discuss these other white people if they had so little impact on the world at large? First off, that statement is blatantly wrong during many epochs of humanity. The Vikings had such a profound influence on the Roman culture, then the European culture, that we're only just recently discovering that reality. European Christian history has had a way of reshaping things so that the "pagan" elements of history are buried or left out altogether. Add to that influence, modern Soviet society with its technological advancements in space exploration and anyone that would claim these other white people are barely worth a footnote would be laughed out of any serious historian's class room.

Let us now begin unraveling the tightly constructed narrative of humanity so that we can see the importance of these other white people.

Chapter 2 Out Of Africa

The narrative of history often changes and is the reason history cannot always be relied upon to help us understand the world around us. History is not only written by the victors as the old expression goes, but more recently, the narrative of history is developed by the political opportunists that have a motive for relating history in certain ways.

While science is still catching up, most people discussing this topic will cite Charles Darwin's theory of how humans may have evolved from apes, specifically African apes. As the scientific community has been operating within Darwin's speculation, they assume that all modern humanity originated in Africa and has spread out from there.

While some models have other proto-humans existing concurrently with the humans out of Africa, such as Neanderthals in Europe and Denisovans in Asia, most of those models claim there was an "infertility barrier" that disallowed crossbreeding among those species and the humans out of Africa, and thus those proto-humans were supplanted by the dominant modern humans migrating into Europe and Asia out of Africa.

All of this requires a great deal of speculation and is not settled science. In fact, there are other theories in play, such as the "multiregional origin hypothesis" which postulates human evolution simultaneously in multiple places at once, and not just in Africa. https://en.wikipedia.org/wiki/Multiregional_origin_of_m odern_humans

A major problem with the Out of Africa theory is that it doesn't explain how the races have so quickly become different than their supposed African origin. Sometimes it is proposed that there was no infertility barrier and that the humans coming out of Africa, interbred with the proto-humans, thus diluting their human gene pool. This theory would fit well with Elijah Muhammad's idea that all races except the blacker races are inferior human specimens.

Mitochondrial DNA analysis is even in dispute as *archaeogenetics* is a rather new field of science and contains within that community, conflicting conclusions. Debate in this field is rife with political pressures to uphold the Out of Africa narrative. For example, DNA research on the so-called "Mungo Man" out of Australia led researchers to theorize that the remains supported the multiregional origin model. This conclusion caused some political upheaval and a reanalysis was done which amazingly enough, agreed with the political conclusion.

Merely questioning the Out of Africa theory by a white person is enough to engender an accusation of racist motivation, as if the white person is only trying to discredit the theory because the white person doesn't want to see his or her ancestors having originated from black people. This kind of political and cultural pressure discourages true scientific discovery.

Nor can it be said, that white people are trying to uphold some white reverse version of the "Yacub History" where it was black and brown humans that were inferior since historically speaking, most white people didn't identify themselves by the pigment of their skin but rather by the region or nationality of their heritage. The tension between so-called white people and "people of color" is a rather newer cultural phenomenon perhaps no older than four or five hundred years. Before that, most humans considered that their various deities created all people, no matter the color of skin. The superiority or inferiority that may have been present among humans was attributed not to skin color but to region or heritage. For example, a black African might be part of a heritage or region that never had a need to build huge sailing vessels. It had nothing to do with some inherent inferiority based on skin color.

Returning to the theory that there was no infertility barrier and that humans and proto- or archaic humans could interbreed. This theory is gaining support as of late and has sometimes been called "admixture". The percentage of supposed archaic human DNA among some human groups is said to be 2-3%. This seems hardly enough to imply that the white and Asian humans were originally black African humans that lost their dark features through interbreeding with these archaic humans.

Why does the author seem intent on making a case that the Out of Africa theory is not as solid as it is presented? Is the author merely trying to justify his whiteness as equal or even superior? Certainly not. All the competing theories, besides perhaps the Yacub History are plausible reasons why there is such diversity between the races.

We have yet to even mention the long held biblical accounts how all humanity derives from Noah and his three sons. How some people claim that black people derive from the cursed Canaan offspring of Noah's son Ham. Or how in Mormonism, the "red skinned" Native Americans are that way due to yet another curse. Further, how the Hadith in Muslim tradition claims Muhammad was "white" though he is typically portrayed now as a dark skinned Arabian. (Sahih Bukhari Vol 1/Bk 8/Had 367,Vol 4/Bk 56/Had 767,Vol 9/Bk 90/Had 342 = https://quranx.com/Hadith/Bukhari/USC-MSA)

The point the author is trying to make is that narratives are in play. Just as the reader might conclude that there has been a concerted effort to diminish if not altogether purge "black and brown" people's contributions to the world, history shows that the pendulum of narrative is swinging. We as honest students of history and science must realize we are being manipulated and try to navigate between the fraud. It is not racist to acknowledge that Egypt is and was different from the southern parts of Africa. Those narratives that appeal to the ancient Egyptian society as evidence of the superiority of the "black race" is part of a planned narrative. Yet, by acknowledging that the Egyptians were Phoenician transplants and not "negroidic" Africans is also not a message of white superiority or a disparagement of black people. It is simply a reality.

The Introgression of humanity is a difficult topic to discuss because even among recent hybridization within humans of differing races, societal pressure is to either ignore the originating variants or ascribe to the person one variant, such as how president Barack Obama is classified as the USA's first "black" president when his mother was white. This harkens back to yet another approach to the admixture of the races called the "one-drop rule" where a person that has ancestry that can be traced to one black person, thus can be classified as black. This hypodescent and hyperdescent method of classifying descendants is akin to the genealogical practice of following the genetic line through the father's line rather than the mother's, but in this case, depending on the motivation of the practice, the person is classified by their admixture race.

This brings us back to the Out of Africa theory. If all of humanity came out of Africa, then are all humans Africans? Do all humans have "one-drop" of African blood running through their veins? Or, if we accept one of the competing theories, humanity evolved in multiple places at the same time from its own strains. Even if the idea is that all humans evolved from apes; it was from apes in Europe, in Asia, in Africa, the Americas and other places rather than from a singular source.

If the reader prefers, they could opt for any of the religious accounts, whether that is the Adamic account in the Semitic texts or the Mashyan account in the Persian texts or some other creation story, the person will still need to reconcile why there are such diverse races of humans.

The Out of Africa theory might be bolstered by the concept of Pangaea, the supposed supercontinent that existed before the current continental configuration. This would imply that Africa was the center of Pangaea and that humanity spread out from there, before the breakup of the singular Pangaean continent. Further, besides the obvious darker skin, the other features of black Africans such as tight curled hair and flared nasal passages might be attributed to long-term climate conditions. The adaptation to the heat, allowing these humans to endure whereas the matted hair and often more profuse body hair of Europeans may indicate adaptation to the cooler climate over time. A great side research is a book called, *"Did God Make Them Black?"* by Isaac O. Olaleye 2003. Olaleye spends a considerable amount of time trying to piece together climate influences on the races.

If Africa is truly the starting point of all of humanity, the next question that should come to mind is the technological deficiency of Africa, historically. The author has engaged in sincere discussions with people that attempted to reconcile the lack of some very basic advancements in Africa by pointing to Egypt or claiming suppression by white colonizers. Both of these answers are false. First, as already pointed out, Egypt, while in the most upper northeastern corner of the continent of Africa, is not for lack of a better scientific name, *"negroidic"* Africa. Egypt's culture is decidedly not anything like Zulu or Bantu culture which do share similarities. Claiming Egypt to prove the technological condition of Africa is like the Druids appealing to the advancements of Rome as their technological heritage. These are distinct cultures with differing historical influences.

Secondly, the idea that Africa as a collective continent lacked some of the more basic advancements in metallurgy and land and sea transport because the Europeans oppressed or stole those advancements from Africa, is false. There is no evidence that before the white man arrived, that Africa had these advancements in abundance, anymore than the Native Americans or Oceanic aborigines had these advancements. It is simply a historical fact. To come along and now insert a narrative as if there has been a multi-generational conspiracy is ludicrous.

It is more likely that if there was an Out of Africa migration either before or after some tectonic shift that dispersed the continents into their present locations, that those humans that left had to adapt to very extreme conditions that caused them to develop tools and concepts not necessary for the humans that remained in the "Edenic" paradise of Alkebulan, the original name for Africa. This theory is more in line with the concept that "*necessity is the mother of invention*". There was little to no need for the remaining humans in Alkebu-land to learn how to smelt metals or dredge out a bay to contain huge sailing vessels.

The author hopes the reader feels like due-diligence was given the theory that of all humanity comes out of Africa. The author has not personally concluded any of these theories and is more apt to go along with Darwin himself when Darwin said:

"…it is useless to speculate on this subject, for an ape nearly as large as a man, namely the Dryopithecus of

Lartet, which was closely allied to the anthropomorphous Hylobates, existed in Europe during the Upper Miocene period; and since so remote a period the earth has certainly undergone many great revolutions, and there has been ample time for migration on the largest scale." – *Darwin, Descent of Man, page 199* (http://darwin-online.org.uk/content/frameset?viewtype=text&itemID=F937.1&pageseq=212)

Add to the almost impossible morass of speculation, the intentional political motivation of narrative making and it's not certain how we can come to an accurate conclusion on the topic of whether humans originated exclusively in Africa or were found among many of the other parts of the world simultaneously.

We next will explore the rise and interconnectivity of the societies in Europe and what has been called Eurasia.

Chapter 3 Eurasians

Maps before the collapse of the Soviet Union, so before the year 1991 often classified everything from eastern Germany all the way east to India as Eurasia. But this demarcation is more geopolitical than it is geographical. Eurasia is a tectonic plate under which the political boundaries reside. That is, there is no physical divide between Europe and Asia. It is all one continent. However, for the discussion not only within this book but historically, even the Greek cartographers considered a distinction between Europe, Eurasia, and Asia as three regions. The dividing line between these regions has not been consistent.

Vast swaths of wilderness, rivers, or mountains have been factors that kept the civilizations of these three otherwise arbitrary regions separated.

Technically there has never been a unified people group called "Eurasians" even though like the *European Union* that acts as a unifying body for European countries, so too is there a little known *Eurasian Union* which is mainly constituted of former Soviet states.

But for our discussion we want to go back even further in time before the European Union and even before the foundation of the United States of America.

As addressed, the Greeks divided the regions into three sections, with overlap of Europe and Asia being Eurasia. This comes from the Greek mythology of Europa and Asia, two princesses. Europe and Asia, as names could also have even older origins as in the Assyrian words "ereb" or "erebu" meaning place where the sun sets, as Europe is west of Assyria and "Asu" which means to rise, thus to the east. Otherwise, no one really knows where these words originate.

Whatever the origin, civilizations were divided into these regions. Too often in our modern times we ignore that these were important distinctions.

Another important word origin or etymology to consider here is the word *Caucasian*. Government document forms often erroneously ask the person to select Caucasian as their race if they are "white". But historically, Caucasians are a people group that live around the Caucasus Mountains primarily in parts of the former Soviet Union.

To call a peach-skin colored person a Caucasian shows a lack of historical and geographical knowledge even if that designation has become acceptable. Just as the word "negro" which is literally the Latin word meaning black is too vague a term to describe entire people groups. The author however has used the word *"negroidic African"* to distinguish between Libyans, Egyptians, and Africans further south than Libya and Egypt. This is consistent with the not so precise words of *"Caucasoidic"* or *"Europoidic"* which are obsolete descriptors. Simply calling people white, black, brown, yellow, and, red people is not representative of humanity's supposed more enlightened views of anthropology yet we continue to use these divisive descriptions.

Back to the Eurasians which included such diverse people groups as the Mongols, the Persians (modern Iranians and Iraqis), and yes, Russians. As a matter of fact, yet another word that has become taboo in modern vernacular is the word, *Aryan*. Aryan was a descriptor for Indo-Iranians. It originally had nothing to do with Nazis. It was the self-designation of ancient Iranians and some Indians much as how the Hebrew scriptures and traditions depict "Jews" as the "Chosen people". The designation is more religious or cultural and did not contain concepts of racial superiority.

These Aryan Eurasians more than likely immigrated from the Northern Caucasus Mountains and settled in Iran and India. See the "kingdom of Alania" for reference. https://en.wikipedia.org/wiki/Alania

Without turning this book into a twenty-five volume history of human cultures, the author wants to whet the readers imagination and curiosity to better connect words with concepts. It is obvious that words become inseparably misused so that they can never again carry their original meaning upon their utterance. Take for example the word "*gay*". While that word simply means joyfully happy, it will forever be associated with the sexual practice of proclivities towards a person of the same gender. The moment a person says, "Aryan" or "negro" the emotions those words bore into our subconscious cannot be reconciled with any amount of historical discussion.

Eurasians as a collective people group are then, often ignored by history. We see them as "those Russians" or as some almost cartoonish characters as the Mongols that in reality still exist. The Aryans and Armenians have been almost completely absorbed into other people groups, at least in our minds. Who are these other white people?

So, what were the Eurasians doing while the Europeans were fighting amongst themselves, then colonizing the New World, including exploiting the indigenous people and bringing African laborers against their will to the Americas?

Like much of the ancient world, Russia had slavery, at least in the form of serfs or "unfree" people called *kholop* which translates most accurately to the southern United States term of "*boy*" when addressing a black slave. The kholop were not African laborers, but instead were "white" people who became slaves through debt or crime or lineage as kholop and their families were sold as property with the lands they tended.

While Russia as a nation did not participate in the Transatlantic Slave trade of Africans nor did Russia colonize Africa, individual Russians did play a part. For example, Alexander Sergeyevich Pushkin which is considered by many to be Russia's greatest poet was of sub-Saharan ancestry. His great-grandfather was an African that was kidnapped by the Ottomans (Muslims) and then presented as a gift to Russian ruler, Peter the Great. Peter freed him and raised him in the court as his godson.

Russia, as part of the other white people didn't view black people as commodities. In fact, Pushkin's story reveals another aspect of African slavery that is often not discussed. While history books in the United States are replete with accounts about the Transatlantic Slave Trade, little is mentioned about the even older and longer existing Eastern or Islamic Slave Trade.

The countries we know today as predominately "Muslim countries" were not always so. As mentioned, Iran and Iraq were strongly Persian with their own non-Islamic cultures and religions, primarily Zoroastrianism.

It is important to discuss Islam because it is obviously part of Asia and conquered or influenced much of Eurasia and Africa. To start history at the moment of European contact with Africa from the 1600-1800s is not history but rather narrative, a tightly constructed propagandizing of history. Why is it so important to depict "white people" as the "devils" and almost completely ignore that Islamic invaders wiped out the rich cultures of Constantinople and replaced it with Istanbul or supplanting Alexandria Egypt which thrived with a mix of Phoenician, Greek, Roman, and Christian culture and turn it into a militant Arabian vassal? Further, the Arabs led raids and conquests into the Maghreb which is a name for western North Africa. The author suspects, Arabs rather than Muslims since many of the invading forces weren't there to specifically extend Islam to Africa. Instead, they were there like any colonizing force, to subdue and exploit the native population.

Much of North Africa was occupied by Phoenicians and Berbers or known in modernity as Egyptians and Libyans. It was these people whom the Arab invaders spent most of their time conquering. The black Africans, further south had little in the way of technological or architectural advances that interested the invaders. The black Africans simply became a supply of cheap labor.

A quote from the New African Magazine shows just how significant the Arab slave trade of black Africans was compared to the more commonly mentioned Transatlantic Slave Trade to the Americas.

"Figures on the Arab slave trade in Africa are hard to come by, but the historian Paul Lovejoy estimates that some 9.85 million Africans were shipped out as slaves to Arabia and, in small numbers, to the Indian subcontinent. Lovejoy breaks his figures down as follows:

Between AD 650 and 1600, an average of 5,000 Africans [annually] were shipped out by the Arabs. This makes a rough total of 7.25 million.

Then, between 1600 and 1800, another 1.4 million Africans were shipped out by the Arabs. The 19th century represented the highest point of the Arabian trade where 12,000 Africans were shipped out every year. The total figure for the 19th century alone was 1.2 million slaves to Arabia. Thus, in terms of numbers, Arabia's 9.85 million is not far behind the conservative estimate of nearly 12 million African victims of the Atlantic slave trade." --
https://newafricanmagazine.com/16616/

Perhaps if the author were a descendant of black Africans, these statements about the Arabian slave trade would not be helpful. All this does is solidify that black Africans have been exploited not only by white people but it seems by almost all other people groups. For further discussion on that sentiment, the reader should review the author's book titled, *The History and Future of Black People*.
https://amazon.com/dp/B08X5343JQ

So, it is clear that the other white people, which in this case are the Eurasian white people of Russia and even the Caucasus Mountains and the Indo-Aryans were not participating in the exploitation of the black or brown-skinned peoples of the world. However, the olive or brown-skinned people of the Arabian peninsula were in fact some of the first to sell black Africans into servitude. Even more, many black Africans were more than happy to sell their fellow black-skinned brothers and sisters to the highest bidder.

It was never about the color of the skin but the station in life. The world needed laborers and if your cultures' skillset didn't rank you with designers of massive cities or huge sailing vessels or advancements in literature, philosophy, and society then you were apt to become a commodity traded to those who were part of those advancements. It is a cold reality.

As we leave Eurasia and return westward to northern Europe, specifically to the Scandinavian region, we absolve the other white people in Eurasia of any "evil white people" actions which Elijah Muhammad might ascribe. Yacub's fictitious gene-splicing aside, these other white people don't fit the narrative.

While the Arabs and black Africans were leading the way in the slave trade of Africans, back in pre-slave trading Europe, the British, the Saxons, the French, and the surrounding areas were experiencing their own invaders. Northmen, or Norse were coming down from their rocky, watery strongholds and pillaging the Christian kingdoms. But the Norse, the Vikings didn't come just to raid. They also had aims to settle in these fertile lands. The Vikings wanted to make this warmer climate with lush green fields their new home. Unlike so many cultures where dirt somehow becomes "holy" or sacred, Viking religion carried its significance in the individual. No matter where the person went, their spirituality went with them. It was not reliant on a specific place nor trinket or icon. Instead of the "bar" and "ben/bin" son-of signification in many cultures, Viking sons were expected to make their own name.

Let us now look at these other white people with a more objective perspective than Hollywood might depict them.

Chapter 4 Northmen

As we move away from Eurasia and back to Scandinavia, we do so because while Russia is part of Eurasia, it was settled by Scandinavians; Northmen, so it makes sense to start with the Northmen and follow their movements both into Europe and Russia.

The lore of the Northmen, also known as Vikings clouds the actual history. Much of actual Viking history must be gleaned from what is called the "*sagas*" (ref: https://en.wikipedia.org/wiki/Saga). The Sagas were primarily written in Iceland after the Vikings settled on that landmass, although there are some sagas written while the Northmen were still in Scandinavia. The Sagas are written in prose, poetic, and historical form and tend to be mixed with a good helping of myth and legend, but nevertheless is where we can learn about Vikings from the Vikings themselves.

Like most Native American history, the Viking Sagas were first oral tales and were not committed to writing until many centuries after the events they relate. So, while the Sagas help us, we must rely on archeological evidence to fill in the gaps. Fortunately, with the thawing of many areas that were not always frozen over, we have acquired a storehouse of Viking artifacts including; weapons, ships, clothing, everyday utensils and of course, human remains. From these, researchers can begin to reconstruct the daily life and collective history of the Northmen in contrast to the Hollywood depictions.

Further, with paleontology and advancements in DNA sequencing, researchers are beginning to see just how far-reaching the Viking influence has been.

While this book is not a book of European history, it is important to note that almost every European country has been influenced by the Vikings. Does this then make the Vikings culpable in the "sins" of the Europeans? The "Viking Age", which may be the best way to term the era of the Vikings' influence, spanned from about 800AD to 1150AD before they were more or less assimilated into Christianized European culture. So, if we consider that the European conquest for power and colonization didn't begin in earnest until about 1096AD with the First Crusade of Jerusalem and marked by Christopher Columbus' voyage to the New World in 1492, the Vikings did not have direct influence on these events.

The Northmen eventually would become known as the "Normans", as associated with "Normandy" made infamous in the WW2 battle fought on its beaches.

Normandy spans an area in France and a part of English isles. From Normandy came William the

Conqueror who in 1066AD marched into England to secure his claim of the throne. With William's reign came a formal end to slavery in England. So, we might see from this, that the Northmen, at least in the person of William did not represent the slaver mindset. (ref: https://en.wikipedia.org/wiki/Slavery_in_Britain#Before_1066)

While some Northmen were busy invading and trading in Europe, another contingency of Vikings were moving eastward. These other Vikings history is recorded in The *Russian Primary Chronicle* compiled by Kievan monks in the 12th century (ref: https://en.wikipedia.org/wiki/Primary_Chronicle). The Chronicle details how three brothers; Rurik, Truvor, and Sineus came from Scandinavia and settled in the region. Rurik founded Novgorod which is considered to be one of the oldest cities in Russia. The word Russia comes from the word Rus which in turn comes from the Finnish word, *ruotsi* for people from Sweden and literally means, "*oarsmen*" – men who row boats. The Viking influence in Russia is undeniable.

Next, we follow the Vikings further west beyond continental Europe and onto new landmasses, first into Iceland and Greenland then to *Vinland*, or North America.

In a document called *Landnáma* or the *Book of Settlements* is recorded many "foundations" of Iceland by various Northmen or Nordic people and given different names including; *Tili*, *Snowland*, and of course *Iceland* due to ice drifts.

Greenland is the other island that was settled by the Vikings. As the reader may know, Greenland was named in a bit of creative false advertising. Whereas as the name Iceland immediately conveys to the would-be immigrant that they are moving to a cold, perhaps barren land, Greenland makes a person think of lush fauna and perhaps even a warm climate.

Greenland did have an indigenous population of Inuits ("Eskimos") when the Norsemen arrived from Iceland but the Vikings did not conquer nor displace them but instead settled on a different part of the island. Greenland is over 21 times larger than Iceland and is the world's largest island, although two thirds of it is covered in icesheets and is thus uninhabitable.

Greenland does not contain the rich Nordic heritage as does Iceland since unlike Iceland, it was founded by an exile, Erik the Red who was supposedly banished from Iceland for manslaughter. Iceland was specifically a colony of the Northmen. Further, Greenland to this day still contains many Inuit placenames instead of the Nordic names common in Iceland. This is in part due to the "Little Ice Age" the engulfed the entire planet between 1300AD-1850AD and also due to the Black Plague which caused a decline in many of the Norse colonies, so much so in

Greenland that Portugal briefly claimed Greenland as its own colony in about 1499, calling it *Terra do Lavrador*. Eventually, by the 17th century the Danes once again claimed Greenland but by 1979 Greenland achieved limited autonomy via the Home-Rule Act. During different times in Greenland's existence, the United States of America proposed to buy the island and as of this writing, 2019 was the latest when President Donald Trump offered to purchase the island. (ref: https://en.wikipedia.org/wiki/Proposals_for_the_United_States_to_purchase_Greenland)

Now we move on to perhaps the most controversial expedition of the Northmen, the exploration of Vinland or the United States of America before Christopher Columbus.

Vinland or Vineland was the name given in the *Vinland Sagas* and implies a land of "vines" or even grape vines and thus is sometimes called "Wineland". These Sagas have contradictory or unsubstantiated details which initially made the claim that the Northmen reached the Americas before Columbus debatable. However, excavation in the 1960s verified that indeed there was a Viking settlement in what is present day Newfoundland Canada. The site is currently called L'Anse aux Meadows but may be the site of the Viking settlement named *Leifsbudir*. (ref: https://en.wikipedia.org/wiki/L%27Anse_aux_Meadow

<u>s</u>) The settlement seems to corroborate the Sagas account that a Viking named Leif Erikson established a colony in Vinland. Erikson is the son of Erik the Red, the Viking that was banished to Greenland.

Another Viking named, Thorfinn Karlsefni Thórdarson seems to bolster Leif Erikson's claim to a settlement called Leifsbudir. The Sagas mention Thorfinn and Leif's brother Thorvald as having encountered the indigenous people of Vinland, which the Vikings called *Skræling* which means "dried-skins" pertaining to the pelts worn by the native peoples. Thorvald was killed when an arrow shot by a native, pierced him under his armpit.

The point of recounting these Viking expeditions to Iceland, Greenland, and then to Vinland is to show that they did not come as would the Spanish and Portuguese to conquer and plunder. The Vikings were not interested in converting people to follow Odin or Thor or any part of the Norse religion as would future explorers come in than name of their monarch and Church. Vikings, if not raiding otherwise wanted to find a new place to settle down or with which to trade.

Our last look at the Northmen are the Teutons. Teutons are sometimes identified as North Germanic people or southern Swedes. The borders of nations weren't as static as they are now. The Teutons seem to be a catch-all name given by the Romans to "tribal" people that dwelled in the forests and mountains. The

Teutons were thus, uncivilized, savages; "pagans" not only in contrast to Christianity which was yet to overtake the Roman world for multiple generations hence, but also pagans to the elite pantheon of Greco-Roman deities. Teutons were the wild folk that needed to be constantly pushed back into their place.

The Romans considered the Teutons such fierce fighters that the Romans had a name for the style called, *Furor Teutonicus* which in turn is where the concept of the Viking *berserker* hails which further establishes the connection between Vikings and Teutons and Teutons as a type of a Viking just as much as are the Russians. (ref: https://en.wikipedia.org/wiki/Berserker)

The connection of the Teutons, the proto-Germanic people to the Vikings takes us back to the original contention that both of these groups come from the common ancestry out of the Aryan or Indo-Iranian Caucasus Mountains region which migrated west until it hit the shores of the Atlantic oceans in Scandinavia. From there, they pushed further south and populated Northern Germany.

Thus, the Northmen come from the east and are not actually Europeans. They then conflict with the Romans in ancient times. During the Viking Age, starting in about 800AD, the Northmen moved from their rocky strongholds to invade and explore the lands of their western neighbors and return to their eastern lands in Russia. Despite the depiction of the Vikings going on rampages of pillaging, they were also looking to settle new lands. Of course, most of the lands they came across already had indigenous populations and so would require an adaptation to those existing cultures. Perhaps the best example of this is in the story of the Viking named Rollo that came to France in 885AD wherein after terrorizing the Frankish people, he secured a peace with King Charles the Simple of West Francia. In exchange for settlement, Rollo and his Vikings would be required to convert to Christianity and pledge to defend the land against other Vikings.

This absorption into the conquered cultures is a repeated theme with the Viking incursions into foreign lands. This is important to note, because unlike later European colonizers of the New World, Vikings often adopted their hosts' culture instead of imposing their culture on the conquered people. It is not to say, that the receiving cultures didn't take on some of the Norse cultural behaviors and practices.

Perhaps the greatest influence on Europe from the Vikings was the opening of trade routes to the East. After the fall of the Roman Empire and the rise of the Muslim domination of the Mediterranean sea, Europe entered a sort of "dark ages" of exposure from the East. The Vikings were most interested in silver from the East.

The Vikings' influence on the societies into which they assimilated has been more subtle but nevertheless enduring, such as additions to the local vocabulary, metalworking, art, shipbuilding and of course trading. (ref: http://www.sourcinginnovation.com/archaeology/Arch 07.htm)

Again, different than European colonizers, the Vikings didn't displace their host cultures, but rather assimilated into them, adding their influences. Some of the more innocuous influences are things such as the tradition of Christmas trees, originally a reference to the Yggdrasil Ash tree upon which Viking god, Odin sacrificed himself. In fact, many of the Christmas traditions were originally Viking concepts harkening back to Yuletide. (ref: https://www.history.co.uk/articles/how-the-vikings-gave-us-christmas)

While the author has barely scratched the surface of Norse history in Europe, it is not the purpose of this book to rehash things the reader can easily find in other sources. It is then not necessary to discuss Lindisfarne nor Danelaw. Any reader that picked up this book because they saw the word *Viking* in the subtitle no doubt is already well aware of those topics. This book is about the Other White people, not just Viking history. But it is hoped something new was added to the readers' knowledge.

CHAPTER 5 COLORS

In the world where the author currently lives, it seems everything is about color, specifically skin color. People are rarely identified by their heritage anymore. This is especially true when speaking of "*white people*". People with peach colored skinned are lumped in one group to contrast with a more diverse group often called "*people of color*" or "*pocs*". The POC group usually includes anyone with a black or brown tinting to their skin but sometimes excludes Asians oddly enough. Asians are most likely excluded by the fact that as a group, they tend to be more successful at assimilation into their host societies and also not apt to highlight any real or perceived discrimination against them. They simply succeed within and despite limitations. For this reason, it seems Asians are often excluded from the POCS designation because they will not heed the narrative that they are supposed to be hostile to all "white people".

Interestingly, as discussed earlier, the "brown" designation includes Latinos which ironically are the descendants of the very Europeans that are accused of all the ills that befell the New World. Perhaps it could be said that the admixture of the aborigines and the Iberian conquistadors is now too convoluted to distinguish where the conquerors end and the conquered begin within the individual "brown" person. But, you'd think that a starting point would be to eschew all things reminiscent of the conquerors. This would include giving up the Spanish language and reacquiring the Nahuatl of the Uto-Aztec for example. Or relearning the Inca cuisine of clay-based sauces or guinea pig jerky. Instead, much of Mexico, Central and South America and the Caribbean still prepares and eats the foods of their conquerors.

With all the present effort to throw off the yoke of the colonizers, it would seem the easiest things to change are the last to be set aside, if ever.

So, instead of recapturing their original culture, many people are manipulated into yet another sort of theft of their heritage. They are diluted into skin color. Whether we are talking about brown-skinned Hispanics or Arabians or darker skinned Africans, each has a unique and rich culture which is being ignored simply to force us to look at the color of their skin first.

It is a disservice not only as an individual to merely see them as their skin color but to the ancestors of these people. Africa is not one country but a set of very different cultures that get mashed into a singular designation based on skin color; black. Now, many "black people" try to get back to their African roots without zeroing in on the specific country or region from which they originate, as if being "African" is monolithic. This sometimes manifests as the person making up what they think is "*African*", including names that really don't have etymology in any African society. Then, if anyone questions or points out this discrepancy, the critic is labeled racist or bigoted.

All of this is said to compare how the same thing is done to "white people". As related, Vikings were "white people" that were very different from the other "white people" of England and France. But even without the mention of Vikings, the difference between white British and white French people is very stark. Or perhaps the author should say, _was_ very stark. After the Schengen Agreement in 1985, which led to the dissolution of the hard borders between the European nations, there has been an ongoing erosion of the distinct attributes of individual countries. (ref: https://www.schengenvisainfo.com/schengen-agreement/) Further, the mass immigration into Europe from Islamic nations and Northern Africa has greatly changed the demographics of every European country, including former strongholds of the Vikings.

There is accusation that all of this is an intentional effort of reverse colonization; to colonize the colonizers if you will. It could even be an effort to "de-white" the so-called white nations. There is a false notion that if the world was comprised of humans of only one color, of a creamy butterscotch, then there would finally be peace between the races. The author calls it a false notion because, humans will always find something to distinguish themselves from each other; whether it is skin color, hair color, eye color, or even very minute differences in shading.

Humans didn't always classify one another by skin color. Rather, a person or group of people were recognized primarily through their religion or geographical location such as Christians versus pagans or "*Mohommedians*" versus the Scythians and so forth. Geographically, the separation might be between the "*hill people*" and the "*people from the sea*". The color of a person's skin was not the immediate identifying factor.

The word *race* doesn't even require a definition of skin color. A group of people might be considered a "*race of giants*" or a "*race of cannibals*" for example. The word race was first used to indicate people of the same language or nationality. Skin color was only one trait upon which race might be based.

In modern times (now and perhaps in some future reader's world), race has become almost exclusively related to skin color, although a person may be accused of "*racism*" if they say anything in opposition to any other person's identities, including skin color, religion, nationality, language, and even sexual practices. In effect, the words race and racism are both nonsensical social constructs.

Ironically, governments claim to be against classifying people by their skin color or any other physical trait but at the same time often require a racial identification on official forms.

Another interesting historical note about color is how economic classes of people saw color. The darker the tint, within the person's own society was seen as a more impoverished person in that the more affluent class of person did not require laboring in the hot sun to darken the skin. This is true among "white people" and "black people". Black people weren't all seen as impoverished, but a black person that was darker than other black people may be seen as the more impoverished among fellow black people.

As the Age of Exploration gained steam and Europeans encountered new people groups, the Europeans began to speculate about the differences and commonalities. They began to focus on what they thought were predispositions of the groups they found. The conclusions were not based on enough evidence but they began to conclude that the lack of technological advancement and the ease at which these people could be dominated had direct relation to their skin color.

One of the earliest comprehensive essays on race as it relates to skin color was by French physician and traveler, François Bernier called in English, "*New Division of the Earth*" written in 1684. Curiously,

Bernier divided the races more by region than skin color and saw one of the four divisions lumping together Europeans and North Africans (Libyans and Egyptians), and Indians. But the most distinctive classification in Bernier's essay is that of the Sámi people as a different "race" than Europeans and even Vikings.

The Sámi inhabit many of the areas we consider home to the Vikings, like Norway, Sweden, and Russia. While the Sámi appear to be a cross between "white people" and "Eskimos" they could easily be seen merely as white. Unlike the Europeans and even the Vikings, the Sámi "white people" never colonized nor raided a foreign land. (ref: https://www.iwgia.org/en/sapmi.html)

So, distinguishing people by the color of their skin is not only the antithesis of Martin Luther King jr's "Dream" speech, it is the exact contradiction of the message of tolerance and diversity. The epitome of diversity is seeing a person as an individual rather than classifying them by some shared trait; be it skin color, religion, nationality or some other difference.

There is instead a perpetuation of division disguised as progress and advancement. Having government organizations and caucuses that specify skin color seems a counterproductive approach towards equality and equity if indeed that is the goal.

In multiple conversations with people with all different skin color shades, the author asked two questions, questions he desires the reader to ask themselves.

1. What is the difference between justice and revenge?

2. When will we know we have achieved racial equality?

Maybe the first can be answered by saying that justice is carried out by a lawful third-party authority whereas revenge is personal retribution but this definition may not be enough. Is justice and revenge the same when both require a recompense commensurate with the violation? That is, the old "*eye for an eye*" moral standard. Who decides when and what payment is equal to the offense? How long and how much must be the payment or punishment until it is satisfied? This question is directly related to the concept that "*white people*" need to pay or go through some sort of reparations, which seem to have no end. Add to that, in this book, we're talking about white people that had no part in the offense.

The second question is even more difficult because the goal is set differently depending whom is asked. The author asked a close relative who happens to be half-white and half-black and the answer was that equality will not happen until all humans are a creamy beige color. This seems not only unlikely but on two fronts an unsatisfactory solution. First, it would eradicate uniquely black and white people. It seems the epitome of racism. Secondly, humans will still find differences to divide themselves even if they were somehow magically all the same skin shade. This merely pushes the issue into other variances such as eye color, hair length, height, handedness or whatever.

The author is not certain either of these questions have a realistic chance of achievability. Even in the best justice system, whether from corruption, blind technicality, or just sheer emotion-driven opinion justice may be lacking.

A public discussion of these two questions before we even broach the transgressions would be a very beneficial movement toward a reconciliation.

As many activists have concluded, there may be no hope for reconciliation. While there are many people of differing skin pigments that live peacefully beside each other in the various nations of the world, it continues to be an issue. The issue is not just a white-black problem. Take the Dominican Republic and

Haiti situation for example. You have an island that is effectively cut in half by skin color. As the author has been to the Dominican Republic several times, he can attest that "black" people do live on the Hispanic "brown people" side of the island but Haiti is almost exclusively black people. Does some UN force need to come in and impose desegregation? Would that work? Is that "justice"?

With the colors of people, come other attributes such as culture. Forcing people to not only accept but adopt another culture within their own is often a one-sided endeavor. This is obvious by how it is acceptable to promote "black pride" or "black history" but would be considered racist to say the same about "white pride" or "white history". Indeed, most white people wouldn't want to celebrate in this way anyhow, since as said before, historically white people have not put a focus on their skin color and instead focus on their religious or national heritage as Irish, British, German, Russian and so on.

It seems that the more achievable goal would be to help people transition from color-based pride and focus to something more tangible and less likely to foment division. A pride in heritages that may overlap thus giving an organic commonality rather than an imposed divisive trigger. We can't really control our color but we can control our interests. Find common interests.

Chapter 6 The System

The previous chapter should have brought the reader to this very real conclusion; that the reason white people don't care to focus on their skin color in the same way black or brown people do is perhaps because white people have been in the dominant position for most of history. Note, the author did not say in the majority, because technically white people are not and were not the numeric majority in many of the places they inhabit. But they have been in control of the system over those places. From this, comes the concept of *systemic racism*. The charge is that the system is "white" so that the default pride and focus is white and therefore does not need to be called "white pride" or "white history" and is why there needs to be a distinction of color for other contributions.

Back to the two questions from the previous chapter, how much of the system would need to be changed so that people no longer think it is a white-controlled system? If black people are only 13% of the U.S. population, would having 13% representation in government, entertainment, culture, and such be equality? Would we need to also equalize areas where black and brown people are dominant, such as some sports or the music industry? Where does all this effort to colorize and de-colorize end?

To carry this concept further, should we hypothetically desegregate not only places like the Dominican Republic and Haiti but Jamacia, Africa, and all of Europe until all those places have the equal mix of white and non-white people? Should there be some UN committee that assesses everything to make certain the system has the correct mix?

Interestingly, the system as defined in the USA as the government, educational institutions, entertainment industry, media, social media, businesses and more have been controlled mainly by the white people who claim other white people are the racists. That is, without getting too political in this book, the "*System*" has been dominated by the Democratic Party for most of the United States' history yet it is the Democrats that accuse the Republicans of "systemic racism". How can those who have been in control of the system longer than anyone, accuse someone else of the very things they have been doing? This is important to the discussion of the "*other white people*" as well. There are a large group of white people, who ideologically do not view themselves and other people as majorities versus minorities. They simply see themselves and other people as people. Does this color-blindness hurt or help the progression to the stated goal?

Changing the system in an artificial way will only breed resentment and perhaps dependence. The attempts at fixing the system by passing policies such as Affirmative Action, or hiring quotas where a company or branch of government has to hire a specified number of various races will certainly lead to animosity and often not put the most qualified people into the positions. Perhaps some reader doesn't care. They simply want to fill the positions and the qualifications will come later. Or they will claim that either the person filling the position is qualified but the system's racism is not acknowledging it. Or that it is understood that the person filling the position isn't qualified because the educational/training system is racist against them. What ever the cause, the solution of looking at color before qualification is a de-evolution of society. This doesn't fix the system but rather creates and equally broken or even more broken system than already exists.

Returning a bit to our political look at the system, what if a large group of white people as represented by a particular political party could convince other people that although they have largely been in control of the system for decades if not centuries, they somehow are not to blame for the flaws of the system? Does it sound like a conspiracy theory?

In 1964, at the height of the Civil Rights Era, Malcolm X was addressing the 80% support that black Americans were giving to the Democratic Party.

"Any time you throw your weight behind a political party that controls two-thirds of the government, and that party can't keep the promise that it made to you during election time, and you are dumb enough to walk around continuing to identify yourself with that party -- you're not only a chump but you're a traitor to your race."

https://www.washingtonexaminer.com/when-blacks-voted-80-percent-democratic-malcolm-x-called-them-chumps

Since 1964, black support for the Democratic Party has swelled to over 90%. Why we might ask, in light of Malcolm X's observation? This is very relevant to our discussion on "the system".

If you talk to Democrat political scientists, they will claim there was a "switch in the parties". Oddly enough, they can only cite one instance where a Republican political adviser suggested the presidential candidate reach out to white people in the south. But did this constitute a radical change from what Malcolm X was saying about the Democratic Party? Did the Democratic Party suddenly earn the support of over 90% of the votes from black Americans? What did the Democratic Party do to earn that support?

What does this have to do with talking about white people the reader may ask? Everything. This is a battle between two types of white people. Malcolm X also said:

"The white liberal differs from the white conservative only in one way: the liberal is more deceitful than the conservative. The liberal is more hypocritical than the conservative. Both want power, but the white liberal is the one who has perfected the art of posing as the Negro's friend and benefactor; and by winning the friendship, allegiance, and support of the Negro, the white liberal is able to use the Negro as a pawn or tool in this political 'football game' that is constantly raging between the white liberals and white conservatives.

Politically the American Negro is nothing but a football and the white liberals control this mentally dead ball through tricks of tokenism: false promises of integration and civil rights. In this profitable game of deceiving and exploiting the political politician of the American Negro, those white liberals have the willing cooperation of the Negro civil rights leaders. These 'leaders' sell out our people for just a few crumbs of token recognition and token gains. These 'leaders' are satisfied with token victories and token progress because they themselves are nothing but token leaders." -- Malcolm X (ref: https://www.globalresearch.ca/what-did-malcolm-x-really-think-about-the-democratic-party/5576198)

When did the white liberal stop manipulating and exploiting black Americans is the important "system" question?

Don't get caught up on party politics. The issue the author is trying to get the reader to see is that there is an ideological divide between white people when it comes to the system. There is a systemic history of some white people seeing non-whites as tokens, pawns, pieces in a game. Has that changed and when did it change?

Malcolm X identified that these certain white people were manipulating black people for their support. These white people would even put black people in positions of power, like having them as their Vice-president for no other reason than saying they have a black person with them, which is the very definition of tokenism. Unfortunately, as Malcolm X also noted, some black people don't care that they are being used in this manner. For these black people it is all about the power and privilege of…well, as the old slave dichotomy goes, being a *"house negro"* as opposed to the *"field negro"*. At least they were up in the house with "Massa". They will take what they can get.

This brings us to the point of this chapter. Among the two ideologies of white people; there is one that wants to just see people as people. This may require not constantly focusing on the past. Not constantly trying to repay for wrongs that some white people did to some black people in the past and just realizing history is history and should be absorbed into who we are as a people rather than rewritten or purged from memory. Then there are the other white people who have systematically looked at non-white people as less evolved and less "equal" to them as white humans. These white people didn't suddenly stop thinking that of non-white people, but instead figured out how to do as Malcolm X said, and use these "savages" to their advantage. Give them just enough. Promise them just enough. Tell them other white people won't help them or don't care about them because those other white people aren't passing laws and policies to "help" non-white people. This perpetual race-baiting game goes on and on.

The author wonders if it is better to treat fellow humans like equals instead of pretending to be their great white saviors, especially when historically, these supposed melanin messiahs are the very ones that were oppressing the non-whites?

Wouldn't it be better to start acknowledging the diverse culture of people rather than the diverse skin shades…well, unless there is an ulterior motive for a person to keep the focus on that difference? To use that difference for political gain. To use that difference to keep in control of the system.

CHAPTER 7 STEREOTYPICAL

So far, this book has been addressing the differences between the races and even somewhat trying to justify and excuse some white people from the stereotypes about white people. Especially because as we have discussed, there are other white people that had nothing to do with some of the negative stereotypes against all white people. Perhaps some reader would say that – given the chance – those other white people would have behaved just like the white people that perpetrated those negatives. Further, that unless these other white people spend time not only berating the guilty white people but also apologizing for their own skin pigment in relation, then these other white people are just as guilty. Never mind that the white people that perpetrated ills against non-white people are no longer here any more than the non-white people that had it done to them. The only fair "reparations" might have come in the 1800s when both groups of people were still living.

Some people might even argue that reparations via blood and loss of life of white people was paid in full. Many of the Northern Union soldiers that fought and died in the United States Civil War never owned slaves, nor were they part of the slave trade yet they died to correct that error.

Moving away from the contention between the races, we now look at white people in general, almost as if there were no other kind of people. Why? Isn't that "racist"? No. We want to examine the difference between the white people to see if there is such a thing as the stereotypical white person. If we inject other races into this examination, it will skew our results. The differences we conclude might be the other races' influence rather than the differences and commonalities between white people.

First, we'll need to list some stereotypes about white people. Where do we find such a list?

Luckily for the reader, this book was written during the Information Age, during a time when there was a worldwide web of data sharing called the Internet. In this era, all sorts of information and misinformation, propaganda and activism can be found. Sifting through all that, the author has come up with a list to present. First, many people see at least two classes of white people.

1. **Middle to upper class white people.**
2. **Poor and uneducated white people.**

These two classes come with their own stereotypes.

But we're trying to ascertain stereotypes common to all white people. Is it possible – especially if we consider white people worldwide?

Some stereotypes, in no particular order might be:

1. **Entitled**
2. **Superior**
3. **Less communal**

The author could have delved into more obscure stereotypes like *"white people can't dance"* or *"aren't as athletic as"* some other group. Or even more negative stereotypes such as *"white people are brutish, condescending and rude"* but these so-called stereotypes are more difficult to prove applicable. If the reader wants to follow that line of reasoning, they might check out this link: https://en.wikipedia.org/wiki/Stereotypes_of_white_Americans

Now, let us return to the three stereotypes outlined.

- **Entitled** – Entitled to what? Entitled to have their views heard in any situation? Entitled to attain certain status or position?

Is this entitlement due to the skin color or the history of their dominance? Like it or not, it has been "white people", from the Romans and Greeks which dominated much of the east and west in their expansion, to the European colonization of the New World. Whether viewed negatively or positively, these "white people" developed the resources and technologies to accomplish these things. Does this fact entitle their descendants to anything?

- **Superior** – How are they superior is the question? As touched on, is there some genetic difference that makes white humans superior to non-white humans? This author does not believe so and has even presented the opposite thinking from Elijah Muhammad and the early version of Malcolm X as an example.

  If there is any superiority, it is through the fact that these "white" cultures were able to utilize technologies that some of the non-white cultures did not yet possess such as beasts of burden, metallurgy, gunpowder (originally developed by the Asians), advanced ship building and more.

- **Less communal** – This stereotype is perhaps the most important one on which we should focus because it is the one least attributed but most likely the difference between the races.

  Where many non-white races have strong communal or tribal bonds, historically white cultures have had less communal focus. It was more about the individual. White cultures often champion the individual, the "*king*" or the "*queen*" or the singular "*hero*" that saved the day or won the war. Whereas non-white cultures often focus on the "*people*" or the "*village*". Whatever is to be done is done through a committee of elders or a group decision.

  This communal approach doesn't often take risks or do things outside the expected group behavior. The action of a group is slower than the impulse of an individual. This communal approach doesn't often do things that dramatically affect change but rather it maintains things as they've always been, the "*tradition of ancestors*".

  Where white cultures have been more communal, those white cultures have ceased to be very distinctive and have been absorbed into other cultures, such as the Christianization and Europeanization of the Vikings. The Vikings were both individualistic but also tribal, almost like the white version of *"Indians"* or Native Americans.

Conversely, where non-white cultures have been less communal, they have tended to have more effect on history.

So, when we look at the stereotypical white person, whether rich or poor, educated or not, from the USA or some other place we might conclude the three stereotypes listed as attributing to some of the other stereotypes someone may think of when assessing white people.

Perhaps the reader won't be satisfied with the author's presentation here. Maybe the reader thinks that the author should have applied to white people, the stereotype of racism, that all white people are hostile towards non-white people in some way. That white people are clinging to their dominance and control of the system. That white people will not allow non-white people to participate in society unless the non-white people "act white".

What does it mean to "act white"? What is "white behavior"?

- **White Behavior** – Another thing said about white people is their behavior, which includes everything from how they teach and learn to how they act towards one another.

There is even a claim that the traditional approach to more concrete things such as mathematics is infused with white behavior. That is, the rote style of memorization is a "white" way of math whereas other cultures may be less absolute and use a more estimated approach. As long as the result is close enough, it is considered correct. By expecting an exact answer to a mathematical equation, the teacher is advancing racism and white superiority. By imposing the expectation of an absolute answer, this supposedly turns non-whites off to mathematical pursuits and disadvantages non-white people in development. https://www.the74million.org/article/can-right-answers-be-wrong-latest-clash-over-white-supremacy-culture-unfolds-in-unlikely-arena-math-class/

Acting white may also be seen in white-to-white interaction. While these observations may actually be more cultural, they are often considered "white behaviors". An example might be how people from a Hispanic culture hug and kiss upon meeting or how loud and boisterous some black people might be in large groups, white people may appear less affectionate and more reserved.

Again, this may have less to do with skin color and more with culture and more with the "*less communal*" heritage of most white cultures. Each person in the white culture is expected to conduct themselves in a tempered manner. To present themselves as an individual and be assessed on their individual behavior.

Another point about white behavior is that a lot of the stereotyping comes from entertainment. For the longest time, most movie and television shows depicted white people in the main roles, so as non-white people observes these representations of white people, this is how they expected all white people to behave. Think of the 1950s TV shows that depicted characters like the Cleavers from the sitcom "*Leave It to Beaver*". The behaviors of the characters were depicted as overly polite, even weak when it came to opposing differing principles. What if the young sons didn't agree with the approach of the older generation? Their verbal response might be "*Well Gee dad, I never thought of it that way*". Rarely were the older people depicted as learning anything from the younger.

In the same way, entertainment has created stereotypes out of the other races by showing black people as poor, subservient or worse, mainly in criminal roles. Fortunately, it has been many decades since either of these depictions of white people or non-white people have been the overarching case in entertainment. However, there seems to be a bit of editorial revenge in entertainment and marketing. You will often see white males in roles, especially in commercials that make them appear buffoonish and even effeminate rather than confident or overtly masculine. Further, there is an effort to pair differing-race couples in commercials so that there is never a typical white family group. The author isn't certain what the motive is behind this, but it is obvious in many cases.

As we conclude with this chapter on stereotypes, the author realizes that he has not exhausted the subject. That was never the intention. The reader is urged to continue the discussion with other people, with articles, blogs, social media posts that cite this work and help other people join this conversation. https://rodericke.com/white

CHAPTER 8 THE FUTURE

How is the author doing so far in this presentation? Are you offended? Outraged? Or are you gaining insight into a topic that is typically off limits for any meaningful discussion? Where do you agree or disagree with what has been presented?

As you think about those questions, the author would like to jump to the future; the future of white people. Not just white people in the USA but worldwide.

There seems to be a concerted effort to "de-white" the world, either by interbreeding or decreasing the white population through more rapid procreation and through displacement through immigration. While some white politicians motivation is more about getting votes and less about replacing the white population, there is a fair amount of what is called "white guilt" running rampant among politicians and other influencers in societies. Any resistance against this effort to dilute white dominance in any area is considered white supremacy and racism.

In an attempt to alleviate the accusation, the author will use immigration demographics of Europe over the last few decades.

The reader can follow along with this assessment in more detail by referencing: https://en.wikipedia.org/wiki/Immigration_to_Europe

The percentage of non-European born citizens in EU countries has dramatically increased in the 21st century. When the total population of immigrants and refugees from Asia and the African continent is 39% of the EU population, adding to that the reproduction of foreign-born people is increasing, the native Europeans will be outpaced in the near future.

Area of origin	Number of immigrants to Europe (millions)	Percentage of total number of immigrants to Europe
Africa	8.9	12
Asia	18.6	27
Europe	37.8	52

Area of origin	Number of immigrants to Europe (millions)	Percentage of total number of immigrants to Europe
Latin America and the Caribbean	4.5	6
Northern America	0.9	1
Oceania	0.3	0.4
TOTAL	72.4	100
Various	1.3	2

This is a breakdown by major area of origin of the 72.4 million migrants residing in Europe (out of a population of 742 million) at mid-2013, based on the United Nations report *Trends in International Migrant Stock: The 2013 Revision*. Source: en.wikipedia.org/wiki/Immigration_to_Europe#Statistics_for_European_Union_27_(post-Brexit)

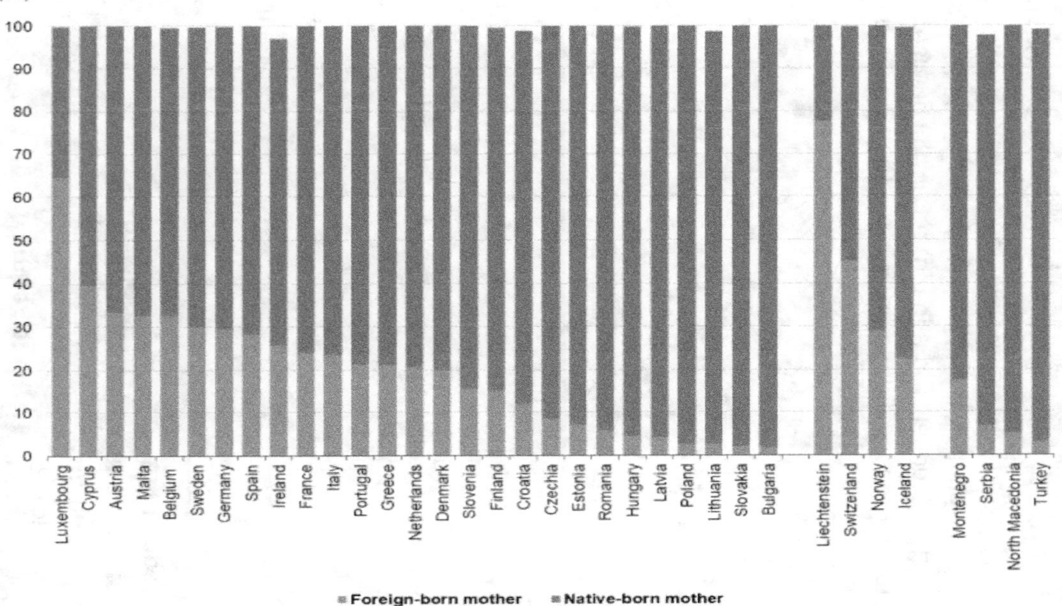
Share of live births from foreign-born and native-born mothers, 2020
(%)

Note: mothers of unknown country of birth are not included.
Source: Eurostat (online data code: demo_facbc)

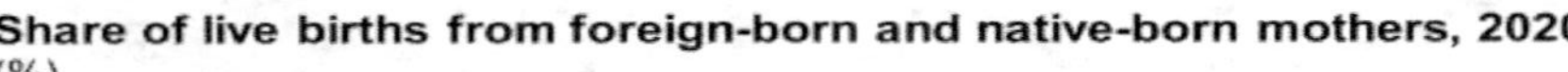

Perhaps the response to all this data is, "*So what? Who cares if the white people in Europe are replaced by non-whites. It is a bit of revenge and reverse colonization.*" This sentiment brings us back to the statement in chapter 5 where we wanted to find the difference between justice and revenge.

Why should a group of people, or an individual within that group allow and sit by while revenge is being perpetrated on them?

There are many that seek this moment, a clash not of cultures but of the races. They seek a race war that will supposedly right the wrongs of the past. To this end, there was even a reimagined historical fiction series made in 2021 called "*Cracka*" that depicted a role-reversal where black people dominated the USA and brought white slaves to the New World. https://youtu.be/Uu2kF8DMyhE

But the division between the races isn't only at the behest of white people. In 1960 there was a secret meeting between the KKK and the Nation of Islam, the premier black Islamists, famous for member Malcolm X. During this meeting, there was discussion how to foment a race war and how to separate the nation once the war destroys the existing structure. This was the beginning of Malcolm X's disillusion with the Black Muslims. He saw they too were merely playing a game.

https://www.politico.com/news/magazine/2020/10/24/malcolm-x-biography-ku-klux-klan-meeting-431657

The Nation of Islam was just as opposed to desegregation and integration as the KKK. Both believed the races should remain separated. The secret meeting was about a plan to make that happen. It obviously failed, at least at the time. To this day, the "newspaper" you might see members of the Nation of Islam selling on urban street corners, called *The Final Call* contains a section that calls for a black nation comprised of four or five states given to them by the USA.

This future that is imagined is not one of integration but of retaliation. It is not enough to make white people second class citizens, they must be eradicated in many of these schemes.

Whether you look into the Apartheid in South Africa, wherein eventually the numerically dominant blacks regained control of the country and now many white ranchers are being attacked. Or you see more recent manifestations of the future in groups like the one led by paramilitary leader "Grandmaster Jay" that is calling for retribution which he knows will lead to war, the future looks bleak.
https://www.theatlantic.com/politics/archive/2021/04/the-many-lives-of-grandmaster-jay/618408/

When white politicians, influencers, and marketers all are working to degrade and help replace any thing that approaches "white culture" or any place within culture for white people, then the future is hostile against white people.

What are the options? White people, as stated are typically not groupthinkers. They are not tribal or communal so it is easier to pick them off as individuals. Any effort they may try to maintain, not of their dominance but of any influence in culture will be depicted as a lone bigot or racist that will not "change with the times".

Another option would be to move further and further away from the subtle race war that is brewing. Move to the suburbs. Move to the rural areas. But as we've seen, this is only a temporary fix. Such an effort is almost pointless in a connected world where the culture war is piped into your community and home. Everything from the supposed background music to a cereal commercial to as discussed, the intentional depiction of white people as dumb or out of touch is a constant volley from the war machine.

The last option would be to join or surrender to the race war. Admit your guilt. Admit the sins of your ancestors and realize your family line will come to an end. The author is not talking about "keeping your family 'pure'", but rather simply that eventually there will be nothing left of the culture from which you come.

Ironically, the race war that was being designed by the Nation of Islam and the KKK has morphed into a larger culture war where sexual practices dominate even racial differences.

The future that the Nation of Islam and the KKK imagine might be just as terrifying to them as the depiction of the Cracka series; one where anyone that does not accede to the sexual and genderless ideologies will become a second class citizen or targeted for annihilation. Does the reader think the author has gone off into a quite conspiratorial corner? Did you read the link about the meetings between the Nation of Islam and the KKK? If these sorts of things were going on in the 1960s at the height we were being told there was no agreement between differing factions, then why do we not think there can't be a designed effort to overthrow the current structure?

During the "*Black Lives Matter*" (BLM) riots between 2020-21 there were groups of white people that voluntarily prostrated themselves at the feet of black people and begged for forgiveness for what their ancestors did to black people in the past.

https://youtu.be/fdX6aVzPgHs

This admission of guilt only plays into the perpetual retribution and revenge mentality against white people. As this book is specifically about *other white people*, would they be exempt from this guilt or is the agenda not really about accuracy in history?

The future of not only white people but society in general is all tied to what happens in the next few decades. Like it or not, many of the metropolises and technological advancements in the world were designed and built by white people. An example of why this fact is important can be seen in South Africa and Zimbabwe where after the control of those nations were handed over to the black majority, they were unready, and not knowledgeable about how the country was able to build and maintain a civilized society. Worse yet, the old adage of "power corrupts" has been on full display as people that previously had little to no power, suddenly had it all.

The issue isn't about whether this power is suddenly turned over to black people or brown people or other white people. The issue is whether the people that inherit society will have the knowledge and ability to maintain it? Does the next generation of whomever it may be, have the skills and curiosity to build and maintain infrastructure like water treatment plants or bridges and such? Does the next generation have engineers to design new infrastructure and repair what already exists?

If the future is given over to people of any color – this book isn't implying non-white people are incapable of technical thinking – can this next generation keep society from collapsing?

The author wrote and produced a 9 minute movie that addresses this question as it follows the thoughts of a lone revolutionary that must reconcile his decisions with the unexpected results.

https://rodericke.com/utopiaundone

CHAPTER 9 NON-WHITE WHITES

A strange phenomenon in classification happens when you ask a person what makes a person black, white, or any other color? The simple and supposedly obvious answer would be the shade of skin, but many people will claim behavior has just as much a role in determining a person's race. If a black person doesn't "act black" or doesn't support black agendas, that person may be classified as not black. This is especially the case when it comes to Latinos and Asians.

News reports may call someone a *white Latino* or *white Hispanic* in an attempt to bias the report. What is often meant by this added classification is that the person isn't white but they behave "white" or support what is supposedly a "white" position. It could also mean the person does not bear traits of being a Latino such as not being able to speak Spanish.

This identification of being a "white Latino" can be self-applied or imposed on the person as a pejorative. https://en.wikipedia.org/wiki/White_Hispanic_and_Latino_Americans

Further, a non-white white classification is often applied to Asians when it comes to college admissions quotas. Since many colleges and universities have racial quotas that typically require a certain percentage of "minorities" to be enrolled, and since Asians often outperform even white students, the intended quota system become skewed where the institution will end up with very few black or Hispanic students because the Asians quickly fill the "minority" requirement. So, by classifying Asians in with white people, this leaves room to add more blacks and Latinos to the system.

As mentioned earlier in the book, Asians also often do not spend as much time concerned with animosity towards white people so the "people of color" status is not always applied to Asians. However, Asians have plenty of historical reasons to be hostile towards whites. This history includes the banning of Asian immigration to the U.S. which included The Chinese Exclusion Act of 1882 which was meant to stifle the competition of Chinese immigrants for jobs and businesses. https://www.archives.gov/milestone-documents/chinese-exclusion-act

It was not just the Chinese, but during World War Two, the U.S. government seized property of second and third generation Japanese-Americans and interred these U.S. citizens in camps. https://www.history.com/topics/world-war-ii/japanese-american-relocation

Even Native Americans, so-called "redskins" can be classified as "white" if they do not show enough hostility towards white people.

There is a reason activists created the classification of "people of color". They need a larger group of "us against them". They need it to be everyone else against the white people and if you are not white but don't join in the animosity against white people, then you are re-classified as white and will be attacked as well. This is the brewing race war that the Nation of Islam and KKK joined forces to foment.

Indians, from India are also often considered "white", not so much because of any alliance with white people but because they are too successful. To the race-baiting activists, if a person is too successful then they must be part of the system that allows and encourages success and if they are part of the system, they too must be defeated.

Another thing that keeps certain groups of people from being considered part of the "people of color" is their history of hostility towards black people. Since, for example Mexicans immigrating to the USA may at some point inhabit the same neighborhoods as black Americans, an inevitable tension develops. There may be competition for living space or employment.

This hostility is often played out in the prison system where gangs of various ethnicities vie for domination.

This hostility among the non-white races can get individuals or entire groups kicked out of the "rainbow coalition" of races.

Just like the actual Rainbow Coalition organization started in 1969 and co-opted by Jesse Jackson in 1984, these race-based activist groups usually become class warfare organizations that are less about racial equality or equity and more about class revenge. This means, no matter what color a person may be, if they are part of the targeted class, they are treated as "white".

Historically, black people that did not automatically support the "black cause" were classified as "*Uncle Toms*" which is a reference to the character in the book written in 1852 called, "*Uncle Tom's Cabin*". The black character in the book is seen as too subservient to white people and therefore the epithet of being an "*Uncle Tom*" if a non-white person isn't hostile to white people.

This pejorative carries over into modern society where even black Supreme Court Justice, Clarence Thomas is labeled an Uncle Tom if he does not actively push judgments in favor of black people. In contrast, Latino-American Supreme Court Justice Sonia Sotomayor once said at a symposium:

"I further accept that our experiences as women and people of color affect our decisions...I would hope that a wise Latina woman with the richness of her experiences would more often than not reach a better conclusion than a white male who hasn't lived that life." (ref: https://www.npr.org/sections/thetwo-way/2009/05/sotomayors_wise_latina_line_ma.html)

Sotomayor was confirmed even though she never tried to do as the article suggests and downplay her real intention and views.

Where one person is berated for trying to transcend their stereotypes of color and class and make judgments based solely on the law, the other person is championed for openly saying they will be biased when applying their judgments.

In this way, Thomas is considered a non-white white and Sotomayor becomes even more "black" than Thomas.

In the course of defining who is part of the non-white coalition, the labels have evolved from negro, to colored, to black, to a multitude of hyphenated titles and now pronouns, but white people, who are not really even white remain simply "white" even if they are actually peach. They are excluded from color and specifically from the people of color as if they are transparent.

The classification of African-American is unlike so many other hyphenated designations. A person is not often simply called European-American, but rather by the specific nationality (ie French-American, British-American, Irish-American). Granted, the main cause is that most black Americans do not know or have not researched their ancestors' country of origin so instead they use the continental preface to American.

Research shows, that most Africans shipped to the Americas came from what became known as the "slave coast" which includes the present nations of *"Senegal, Gambia, Guinea-Bissau and Mali; and west-central Africa, including what is now Angola, Congo, the Democratic Republic of Congo and Gabon"* and also Ghana. Interestingly, at least to the author the source article also seems to quickly gloss over the fact that of all the slaves shipped to the New World region, only 3.6% were sent to the United States. The larger percentage of African slaves were sent to the "Spanish" and "Portuguese" regions such as the Caribbean, South America, and Brazil yet it is the United States that must constantly answer for the

blight of slavery. (ref:
https://www.history.com/news/what-part-of-africa-did-most-slaves-come-from)

These South Americans and Brazilians are often considered part of the people of color even though they had the largest impact on the darkest of the POCS.

This brings us to a humorous or offensive situation where space and electric vehicle mogul, Elon Musk who was born and raised in South Africa is technically an "African-American". At the time of this writing, Florida governor Ron DeSantis upon hearing that Musk supported DeSantis for president said he was always happy to have African-American support. This is offensive to people that have spent a generation making this title their own. (ref:
https://www.miamiherald.com/news/local/news-columns-blogs/fabiola-santiago/article262576652.html)

This leads us to a further issue which is the word, *appropriation*. It has become taboo for a person from one ethnic group to not only wear a costume that may be part of another group's stereotypical heritage, such as a sombrero for Mexicans, but it has become a social offense to appropriate anything that my seem like it belongs to another ethnic group such as dreadlocks only for black Jamaicans. This insistence that these stereotypes belong to only specific races simply reinforces the stereotypes of which many civil rights activists previously sought to undo. Now, these stereotypes are being embraced and staunchly guarded by the same people or the children of these people that just a generation ago tried to transcend them.

The last topic of this chapter is about the subtle incursion of non-white whites into Africa. Whether we're talking about the semitic Arabian colonization of much of North Africa or the more recent property and business acquisitions by Asians in Africa, Africa is once again seeing its indigenous population displaced to almost second class, by non-white whites or people not typically included in the POC classification.

Even though this book does cover a large amount of anthropological and ethnographic research, this book obviously is not an exhaustive review. The author urges the reader to expand on this content but beware it is rife with activism that has agendas and narratives to maintain.

The classification of non-white whites is fluid and appears to change depending on political allegiances. The next chapter will peer into some of these political alliances and whether they are helpful or hurtful, not only to the other white people trying to distinguish themselves but to the entirety of the human experience.

CHAPTER 10 WHITE AGENDA

Is there such a thing as a white agenda? An effort to advance the cause of white people? If so, what does that agenda entail and who is pushing it?

As covered already, most white people don't think of themselves in terms of color but rather as nationalities, religion-adherents, or individuals without much affiliation with any specific group. This is part of that "*less communal*" stereotype typical of most white people.

Has there ever been a white agenda? What about the Nazis in the 1940s? Books and movies depict Adolph Hitler and the Nazis as the epitome of the white agenda; of advancing white people over non-whites. Modern racists will gravitate towards Nazi symbols and even tattoo their bodies with swastikas in an effort to convey their hatred for non-whites or at least for Jews. (Jew's are ironically often categorized as white by the POCS)

The Nazis promoted a reimagined Aryan race. As previously stated, Aryans came from a region near India. The Nazis also opposed other white people, like the Polish, the Slavs, and the Russians. So, it wasn't about white superiority but rather about the promotion of a specific version of white people, Aryans, which the Nazis borrowed from the Indians just as they borrowed the swastika symbol. Further, Hitler was initially more interested in getting revenge against the Allies which had levied heavy retributive and punitive measures against Germany's participation with the Central Powers in World War One. He saw, at the heart of his focus, Jewish bankers and lawyers which was expanded to all Jews.

Calling someone a Nazi or Hitler has become a pointless catch-all attack which doesn't seem to understand the historical realities of that group or man, especially since left-wing leaning people or groups will often accuse right-wing people or groups as being Nazis – when the FACT is, the Nazi party was literally called the *National Socialist German Workers' Party*. Socialism is a leftist ideology.

To find something that approaches a white agenda, we need to go back further to political parties in the United States.

This book has already touched some on slavery and white European involvement with slavery so the author will not belabor that topic here. If the reader is interested in a more detailed examination of the history of black people, they can read *The History and Future of Black People* https://rodericke.com/black.

So, without rehashing too much, let us simply say that African labor was more about needing cheap workers as evidenced by the fact Irish "slaves" were also brought to the USA for that purpose. The white superiority complex came later, most likely as a means to justify and reconcile what one group of humans was doing to another group of humans. There originally was no white agenda in slavery. It was business, as cold as that sounds.

As time went on, those justifying what they were doing started seeing it as their "destiny" to build a new world, even if that meant using the forced labor of other people.

MANIFEST DESTINY

Ironically, it was Irish newspaper editor John O'Sullivan who in 1845 coined the term *"manifest destiny"* to promote the annexation of Texas. Ironic, because as stated, Irish people were often used as slaves and indentured servants during the early days of the British colonies in the New World.

Before we get to what Manifest Destiny means, let us look at O'Sullivan. He was a member of the Democratic Party. An advocate of president Andrew Jackson's philosophy and policies, which include most infamously harsh actions toward the Native Americans to bring them to submission to the government. All of this fed into what is called Manifest Destiny which is the concept that God had destined that the colonists of America were to dominate the entire continent and perhaps the entire western hemisphere and implement their ideas onto the indigenous populations.

It is important that the author noted that O'Sullivan was a member of the Democratic Party because other prominent Americans such as Abraham Lincoln, Ulysses Grant, and the Whig political party opposed Manifest Destiny. (ref: https://en.wikipedia.org/wiki/Manifest_destiny)

Here is where we begin to see the real birth of the idea of the white agenda or as sometimes referred, *American Imperialism*. If we are going to be faithful historians and learners of truth, we will need to wade into politics a little in this section of the book. Political parties are not merely slogans but groups of people with shared ideas that get together in an attempt to implement those ideas. At the point of Manifest Destiny, you had one political party who believed it was their duty to implement this idea and you had another political party that oppose the concept.

Trying to sift through what was meant by the concept of Manifest Destiny, often gets conflated and confused by modern historians who will claim ideas like *American Exceptionalism* or *America First* concepts are merely form of Manifest Destiny. This is untrue. As stated, the Whig Party which morphed into the new third party called the Republican Party, opposed Manifest Destiny but advocated leading the world by example rather than by imposition. We may be able to understand this distinction more recently in the difference between the United States being an example of a free and well-functioning Republic and the United States actively trying to engage in "nation building" and exporting "democracy" by interfering in the development of other countries. One version is the idea of people of the Whig/Republican Party and the other is the idea of the people of the Democratic Party.

President Ulysses Grant, who was president a few terms after Lincoln said of the concept:

> **"I was bitterly opposed to the measure [to annex Texas], and to this day regard the war [with Mexico] which resulted as one of the most unjust ever waged by a stronger against a weaker nation. It was an instance of a republic following the bad example of European monarchies, in not considering justice in their desire to acquire additional territory."** (ref: https://wwnorton.com/college/history/america7brief/content/multimedia/ch14/research_01d.htm)

What the author is trying to do is establish not only the origin of the concept of the white agenda also known as white supremacy but its connection to a specific political party. If we can view the Nazis as advocates of a white agenda, then what other ideological groups are also advocates of it?

The group that opposed Manifest Destiny were so adamant against it that they said of those who advocated it:

"that the designers and supporters of schemes of conquest, to be carried on by this government, are engaged in treason to our Constitution and Declaration of Rights, giving aid and comfort to the enemies of republicanism, in that they are advocating and preaching the doctrine of the right of conquest" (ref: https://en.wikipedia.org/wiki/Manifest_destiny#Etymology)

Yet, Manifest Destiny continued to guide much of the policies and agenda of the Democratic Party even into modern times.

Again, there is two competing ideologies that began to be implemented early on in American history; one was a ideology that European descendants were divinely or at least superiorly through DNA are supposed to impose their ideas on other people. The second ideology is one where people believe that simply by the fact that they have tried to follow the examples not only of "white people" but of all of human history, of all people in establishing the most beneficial concepts for a healthy and productive society but not force people to adopt these ideas but rather consider the ideas.

This ties back into what Malcolm X observed about white people:

"The white liberal differs from the white conservative only in one way: the liberal is more deceitful than the conservative. The liberal is more hypocritical than the conservative. Both want power, but the white liberal is the one who has perfected the art of posing as the Negro's friend and benefactor; and by winning the friendship, allegiance, and support of the Negro, the white

liberal is able to use the Negro as a pawn or tool in this political 'football game' that is constantly raging between the white liberals and white conservatives." – (ref: https://www.globalresearch.ca/what-did-malcolm-x-really-think-about-the-democratic-party/5576198)

What Malcolm X was really seeing is the dispute between the two ideologies. This dispute came to a head during the American Civil War yet continues to rage as the division among the political parties.

There was no switch in the parties where now the Democratic Party is trying to help the non-white races. Instead, the white Democrats are still trying to impose their ideas on people. This is most clearly seen in the 2020 statement by then presidential candidate Joe Biden who told black Americans that if they *didn't vote for him, then they aren't black*" as if their best interests are wrapped up in the Manifest Destiny interests of his ideology.
https://youtu.be/jhcgmwj3NAc

The Democratic Party presumes superiority and control over those it thinks it represents and if those people dare to not support the party, then as Biden said "*you ain't black*" or whatever demographic the party assumes should support it by default.

The other white people, the other ideology may seem like it is counter to helping "black people" or some specifically defined demographic, but in reality, the other ideology attempts to see people simply as people. There is no *Manifest Destiny* to push "democracy", groupthink, mob rule, or cliquish cancel culture to the world. Instead, there should be an effort to model and example what all humanity is moving towards; a freedom and a liberty of thought and competition of ideas the pare away negatives and leave in its place, not a "white agenda", but a human agenda for all people. True progress, true progressivism is more and more individualism not more sectarianism.

CHAPTER 11 ALL PEOPLE

Returning to the Vikings, they often called their god, Odin, the All Father or *Allfather* as one word. Like many religions, they assumed their god is the creator of all people. When the Vikings encountered other religions, they were very curious how to reconcile those other religions with what they thought about god and reality. Their immediate response was not an attempt to eradicate or force other religion adherents to convert. They often wondered how the Christian god was also the Allfather. How could this depiction of apparent weakness and failure, nailed to a board also be the strong and mighty Allfather in their religion?

Viking exposure to Islam is less documented but one account contained in a journal penned by Ahmad ibn Fadlan, a 10th-century traveling Muslim tells of a conversation between two Muslims and a Viking where the Viking called the Muslims "*idiotic*" for burying their dead where vermin and insects can desecrate the body rather than cremating them as does the Vikings. The encounter was most likely with Russian Vikings. (ref: https://en.wikipedia.org/wiki/Ahmad_ibn_Fadlan#Account_of_the_Rus')

It was this open and tolerant expression of their faith towards Christianity and other religions that would eventually be the Vikings' downfall, as these other white people were assimilated into the white people of Europe and Christianized.

Ironically, the example of Viking governance which boasts to be the longest running parliamentary system in the world is called *The Althing*. This form of government was established in Iceland in 930AD and allowed all free men to attend and interact. It was not a democracy or a republic but did have a grand egalitarian sense. While all free men could attend, those with more importance obviously carried more influence on the final result of the law-making discussions.

Iceland, as mentioned was founded differently than many of the expansions of Europeans.

"[Vikings that] first settled Iceland at that time did not come as part of a planned migration, a political movement, or an organized conquest. Unlike many later European explorers and colonists, Norse explorers and settlers were not acquiring territory for sovereigns or for established religious hierarchies.

Viking Age voyages into the far North Atlantic were independent undertakings, part of a 300-year epoch of seaborne expansion that saw Scandinavian peoples settle in Shetland, Orkney, the Hebrides, parts of Scotland and Ireland, the Faroe Islands, Iceland, Greenland and Finland." (ref: https://www.medievalists.net/2013/12/the-icelandic-althing-dawn-of-parliamentary-democracy/)

Iceland was a colony that did not displace an indigenous people. It was for all people, not just the noble or the monarch's handpicked nor even the prison nation of Australia where Britain sent convicts.

These other white people didn't look at their skin color and decide they were superior or try to implement some Manifest Destiny onto the rest of the world. They didn't dictate who was black or brown or red or yellow or even white by whether those people behaved a certain way or lived up to some stereotype or had hostility towards some other skin color. It was a society for all people, by all people.

When we approach the current times, we must look through the lens of reality and see if we are being manipulated by the ideology that advocated the white agenda and the Manifest Destiny or whether we experience our own *ah-ha* moment as did Malcolm X when he realized all white people aren't "devils". In fact, that all people of any color can exhibit traits of devils or angels.

This entire book has been about not just other white people but about seeing people as people. To finally transcend the race war. To leave behind Darwin's subtle biological superiority of one race over another.

The Allfather or the Universe, with the reality that humans were and are at different stages which can easily be learned and passed around. That progress need not end with one generation.

These other people are all people.

When we look at the totality of human history, we conclude that we have been progressing toward a liberty that is almost anarchy but an anarchy with order and mutual respect. The problem is, on one side there are people that will impose upon and try to manipulate people who want that level of freedom. On the other side, there is what religion calls, "sin" which in base terms is simply greed. Greed will cause one human to steal from other humans. This theft is a robbery of not only possessions but of dignity. Rape is theft of someone's personhood. This greed would never allow for a peaceful anarchy where people mind their own business. Gangs of greedy people would come with violence to take whatever the peaceful individuals have built or acquired. This is the reason for the American Constitution that attempts to articulate and enshrine into law, the epitome of human advancement; individual rights.

We the People of the United States, in Order to form a more perfect Union, establish Justice, insure domestic Tranquility, provide for the common defense, promote the general Welfare, and secure the Blessings of Liberty to ourselves and our Posterity, do ordain and establish this Constitution for the United States of America. – Preamble to the U.S. Constitution

This document attempts to articulate all of human history, of all people. Humans, even in societies that are more communal want tranquility, security, wellness, blessings, and liberty for themselves and their children. It is what the Vikings sought when they left the cold shores of Norway to find lush ground to grow crops and families. It is what the Europeans sought when they left the monarchs' protective robe and went to a wild land. We have to imagine, that even through the pain and sorrow of slavery, the African found themselves in a New World that would eventually allow them to be and do things their ancestors never could. Not that the African should be "thankful" to white people for slavery. The author is certainly NOT saying that, but that whether it is God, the Universe or merely fate; had the Africans been left in Africa to live quietly among their tribes, Africans would have had less influence on the rest of the world. African descendants have gone on to greatly influence the world through inventions, music, sports, and many other areas. Even apparent "bad" things work for the good of people.

This all people coming together in one place is not a repetition of the Tower of Babel wherein that biblical account, human ego thought it to be equal or superior to God. Hopefully, we realize we are flawed in that we will be greedy, even if for mere self-preservation. What parent would not steal or perhaps even kill to preserve their child's life? It is simply human nature.

This all people does not require a monolithic decolorization of the races. That isn't at the heart of our problem. Even building a classless society is not the solution. We will always divide and also always come together. The politicians manipulate even this about us humans. They exploit us with every crisis. They appeal to our compassion. They inflame our emotions. They play us against each other. The sooner we see this, the sooner we can get back to that advancement of humanity, of all people.

Instead of trying to say this group of people are better than some other group, let us consider the contributions from each. Take pride in all people rather than divisively ascribe a month to a specific color of people.

As Martin Luther King jr remarked in his famous "I have a Dream" speech:

"I look to a day when people will not be judged by the color of their skin, but by the content of their character."

This was the goal for a long while but now we live in a world where if we do not see color in everything, then we are considered racist. If we say "all lives matter" instead of just "black lives matter", then we're told we are not recognizing that we must focus on a specific group because it is their lives that are under attack.

But under attack by what and by whom? If it is by a system, then the question is more about what is the system and who has been in control of it?

Some people will argue that King wasn't advocating "color blindness" but rather a focus on character *and* color. That people would first see the person's character then their color. But too often today, the message of so many social justice warriors is one of color first. They will say that the opposite of racist, isn't "not racist" but rather "anti-racist" in that a person against racism needs to be actively fighting racism. The problem is, many so-called anti-racists are actually the most racist against other racists but their own. We've discussed how some "POCS" will re-label people as "white" if they do not actively attack white people or if they appear to not support the "black cause". Rather, an anti-racist is someone who does not see race, is against seeing race.

As we conclude this book, we should then appreciate and celebrate real diversity, not agenda-driven efforts of revenge and self-loathing. Real diversity is not one sided. It is not about promoting one people group over another in an attempt to equalize or equitize. Real diversity appreciates and celebrates all people. It highlights all people. It moves away from dividing people and constantly inflaming people.

We must recognize and fight back against those people that would de-colorize us and turn us all into drones and bullhorn mimicking cheer-squads that pump our fists into the air while chanting some self-defeating protest.

Whether black, brown, yellow, red, or white we are all people; humans that have and continue to contribute to the existence of all people.

There is nothing more racist than constantly seeing race, constantly seeing color just to categorize and classify each color differently as superior or inferior, as guilty or innocent. We are all colors. We are all people.

About The Author

RODERICK EDWARDS is a multi-genre author that was adopted at age 4 and found his birth family at age 50. A lifetime of being an outsider has afforded him the unique opportunity to see human behavior as if he were examining it from another planet.

Whether he is writing a Microsoft Excel help book or an autobiography or a fictional tale of a person on a deserted planet, all of his books come with this special perspective that cannot be duplicated by another author.

Every person that reads a Roderick Edwards book is treated to an almost personal one-on-one conversation with Roderick.

Find out more at
amazon.com/author/roderickedwards

Or visit rodericke.com

OTHER BOOKS BY RODERICK
rodericke.com

SEE ALSO, many of these titles are available as AUDIOBOOKS!!!

audible.com/author/B07B9R59Q2

CAN I ASK A FAVOR?

If you enjoyed this book, found it useful or otherwise then I'd appreciate it if you would post a short review on Amazon. I do read all the reviews personally so that I can continually write what people are wanting.

If you'd like to leave a review then please visit the link below:

amazon.com/author/roderickedwards

Thanks for your support!